# Not
Politically
Correct

NOT Politically Correct

A Field Guide to Surviving the PC Reign of Terror

▶▶

By RIC DOLPHIN

Illustrations by CAM

STEWART
HOUSE

Copyright © 1992 by Ric Dolphin
Illustrations copyright © 1992 by Cameron Cardow

All rights reserved. The use of any part of this publication reproduced, transmitted in any form or by any means, electronic, mechanical, photocopying, recording, or otherwise, or stored in a retrieval system, without the prior written consent of the publisher – or, in case of photocopying or other reprographic copying, a licence from Canadian Reprographic Collective – is an infringement of the copyright law.

Canadian Cataloguing in Publication Data

Dolphin, Ric
   Not politically correct: a field guide to surviving the PC reign of terror

ISBN 1-895246-32-6

1. English language - Social aspects - Humor.
2. Euphemism - Humor. I. Cam, 1960-
II. Title.

PN6178.C3D76   1992   306.4'4'0207   C92-094807-3

Book design: Counterpunch/
       David Vereschagin

Cover illustration: Cameron Cardow

Printed and bound in Canada

Stewart House
481 University Avenue
Toronto, Ontario
M5G 2E9

Table of Contents

Disclaimer

This book has been printed on non-recycled, chlorine-bleached white paper produced from timber clear-cut by non-unionized child laborers in the Amazon Rainforest, then shipped in leaky oil tankers that stopped en route to driftnet-fish for whales.

Not
Politically
Correct

Preface to the First Edition

You once had a schoolteacher you were convinced was designed by sadistic space aliens, space aliens who, perhaps through some crazy fluke (or a nighttime sperm theft) possessed just a dash of Teutonic blood. You know exactly what I mean. This creature was eternally 55-years old, had a tweed and wool exterior, smelled of mothballs, and listed, microscopically, backwards as it advanced upon you, enunciating its words with clicks and hisses, never smiling unless to acknowledge a mathematical paradox – and then smiling only a thin, cold, Germanic smile, little more than a whirr of gears really, before proceeding into the next *segment of the lesson.* Might have been female. Who could really tell?

Perhaps you wondered what sort of a civilization would impose this creature on you: a creature so sexless and joyless, so devoid of humor and juice that it couldn't even become irrational. When defied, it would pause only ever so briefly, as if to tackle a slight surge in its read-only-memory, then assign a visit to the principal, or a detention, all with the rigidity of a crude computing machine. *Click. Whirr.*

Well, whatever kind of intelligence was behind such creations

had a long-range plan. For these things have multiplied alarmingly in recent years. (One shudders to visualize the sorts of reproductive procedures involved.) Some people posit that these grim repeaters represent the final, drab adult stage of the sixties college radical. It goes back farther and deeper than that. But whatever the genesis, we suddenly find ourselves surrounded by these horrors – no longer just in the schoolrooms and libraries, but everywhere decisions are made and minds are shaped: universities, courts, government, publishers, television, newspapers, "task forces" (especially task forces).

In the last couple of years, Science, while stopping short of proving alien origins, has recognized the group as a brand-new genus. It has been assigned the name "Politically Correct" or "The Politically Correct Movement." PC for short.

So we have a label (thank you, Science), but do we really know the enemy? What is the ultimate mission of this rogue strain? Their *modus operandi* is certainly clear: making all of mankind's existence as nasty, brutish and long as their own (*Put out that cigarette!*). Inside sources reveal that these agents of gloom pose a much bigger threat to our species than the hole in the ozone layer or the Greenhouse Effect. For they won't give us merely a mela-noma or an orange grove in Tuktoyaktuk. These PC techno fiends threaten to turn us into themselves. If they're successful in their mission, who will be left to compose obscene limericks or look after our pets?

I mention pets because of course there won't be "pets" any more, there will only be *non-human companions,* quite possibly the beneficiaries of *affirmative action* regulations awarding them *equal status* with the head of household. (The jargonistically challenged can find handy definitions in the glossary at the end of this book.) Our children are already being taught that there are no more crip-ples, merely *physically challenged;* no more beautiful or ugly peo-ple, no stupid or smart people, no black or white people . . . For in the circuitry of the PCers, differentiation along good, bad or obvi-ous lines is *unacceptable* (their most favorite word of all). You remember how that teacher would methodically browbeat you into rolling your French "r"s until your tongue went into a drooling spasm? Well, her heirs are now browbeating everyone about every-thing. *I'm sorry – click – But that word is un-accept-a-bull – click,*

> ## There won't be "pets" any more.

click. Please select a gender-neutral, non-lookist, non-ageist, environmentally friendly alternative – whirr. . .

To what end? Science isn't sure (you jabber-brained pullet, Science). We can only guess what's to become of the intellect or the sexuality or the traditions and beliefs, or indeed the configuration of the underwear openings of the population at large. Under the new regime, for example, boys can no longer be boys, and girls certainly cannot be girls. That would be *sexist*. (And there is nothing more sexist than biology.) However, girls can't be boys either. That would make them *paternalistic* or *patriarchal* or something. But its all right for boys to be girls – whatever girls are exactly . . . See? No, you don't. But (*click, whirr*) you will.

As for history, well that has pretty well been cancelled, since it was both created and written by people – white men and worse – not at all to the tastes of these alien Pecksniffs. In fact, Civilization itself, with its tendency to approve of the strong and fit, is *not at all acceptable*. As you probably already know, PCers have a special affinity for the weak and the dispossessed, the socially unattractive and the sexually confused – just as that teacher liked the friendless

As for history, well that has pretty well been cancelled.

fat girl in the front row with the pimples and the sinus problem (*So easy to mold! So grateful for the assistance! An instant foot soldier! – click, click, click, achtung!*) Primitive civilizations are especially attractive (*So little deprogramming necessary*), instantly accorded noble-sounding titles in the PC lexicon (*founding peoples!*) and even allowed to keep practising their religions – no matter how tree bark-oriented – without fear of the derision heaped upon such *patriarchal and hierarchical superstitions* as, for example, Presbyterianism.

Most of us started to notice the spread of PC outside the classroom long before we had a name to for it. While working as a reporter for a small daily newspaper north of Cleveland in the late 1970s, I remember a clammy representative of Amnesty International once sidled up to my desk and whispered in my ear intelligence on crushed testicle victims. Quickly crossing my legs, I wondered what possible good could a story in my piddling paper do to reduce far-away torture. Since then I've learned that political correctness has nothing to do with logic, common sense, or even the so-called

Primitive civilizations are especially attractive.

over-developed social consciences of its perpetrators. No, it's just the plain inscrutability of those aliens again, as they breed unfettered and recruit easily programmable lieutenants, especially those with a penchant for the garb of the 1960s and a distrust of anything attractive to the eye or pleasing to the senses.

The American philosopher John Searle said the PC movement started to get out of control after "the migration of radical politics from the social sciences to the humanities." The result of that migration is a hellacious gumbo of philosophies. Marxist-tinged theories of "deconstructionism," "structuralism," and "post-modernism," spiced with a bit of witchcraft and New Age whimsy, are seeping into classrooms, law courts and bureaucracies (especially bureaucracies with an affinity for the word "caring"). There is no longer to be such thing as objective truth. Everything is political, everything has a hidden agenda, and the hidden agenda of all Western thought and deed is *oppression and discrimination. (whirr . . . click . . . heidegger . . . heidegger . . .).* When people like me start telling you about the wicked aliens who are behind all of this, well, heck, we're just a bunch of *sexist, racist, paternalistic, hetero-*

> ## Everything has a hidden agenda.

centric, Neanderthal, white males -clickety-clickety-click. No doubt we'll be punished. One can only hope there'll be someone around to whisper word of our punishment into some small-town Nicaraguan newspaper reporter's shell-like ear.

The mass media – all tucked away in some hotel bar for the previous ten years – finally started noticing PC, primarily on campus, in late 1990. *US News and World Report,* in its December issue, sounded the alarum, saying, "Affirmative action, busing, gay rights, women's studies, the PLO, animal rights, bilingualism, the self-segregation of blacks on campus and censorship in the pursuit of tolerance are all politically correct. The following are not PC: the SAT, doubts about abortion, Catholics, wearing fur, any emphasis on standards or excellence, and any suggestion that gender and ethnicity might not be the most overwhelmingly important issue of the modern era."

Newsweek, Atlantic, The New Republic followed soon afterwards. *New York* magazine coined the phrase "new fundamentalists", and before you knew it, a new one was being coined every month – "ayatollahs," "silencers," etc. – although the closest we got to aliens was "Moonies." By May 4, 1991, the concept of political correctness arrived good and proper when George Bush gave it presidential utterance in a commencement address to the University of Michigan in Ann Arbor. "What began began as a crusade for civility," he said, "has soured into a cause of conflict and even censorship." He had better watch out for his testicles.

Maybe it's too late. If you saw the movie remake of *Invasion of the Body Snatchers*, you'll remember how those poor souls already duplicated by the aliens identified those still in possession of their minds by pointing and issuing a sound similar to that of a pterodactyl being slowly dipped into an active volcano. The new body snatchers, the PCers, the multifarious descendents of our robotic teacher, operate in much the same way. They point. Their eyes bug out. And issuing forth from their pinched and antic faces comes the triumvirate invective: *Paternalistic! Fascist! Sexist!*

The time has come to take stock of the alien fiends amongst us. Know the enemy and he is yours. Which is what this field guide is all about.

Etymology

The revised (1991) Random House Webster's College Dictionary, defines "political correctness" as "marked by or adhering to
a typically progressive orthodoxy on issues involving especially
race, gender, sexual affinity or ecology." The New York Times's
language columnist William Safire traced the term's use in its
modern sense back to December, 1975, when Karen DeCrow
(sic), then president of the National Organization of Women,
used the phrase (unironically) in response to criticism that
feminism was only for WASP women. She said that NOW was
in fact moving in the "the intellectually and politically correct
direction." The National Association of Scholars, an anti-PC
organization at Princeton University, traces the term back to the
American black radical Angela Davis who, in 1971, provided the
definitive answer to the often asked question, why won't PCers
ever listen to the other side's point of view? "How can there be
an opposing argument to an issue which has only one correct
side?" asked Davis. She and her fellow Marxist radicals lifted

the term from the works of Chairman Mao Zedong, whose Cultural Revolution, coincidentally, also presaged the re-education methods of today's PCers. In a 1963 thought, later collected in his famous little red book, the Chairman asked, "Where do correct ideas come from?" His answer, as fresh today as ever: "They come from social practice and from it alone."

THE SPECIES

▶▶▶

The following field guide, with its useful illustrations, will provide some idea of the varieties at large. Be aware, however, that interbreeding is common, and the characteristics of one species within the genus are, inevitably, shared with others.

▶ The Boyishly Correct...

▶ cry.

▶ proudly declare themselves feminist.

▶ hyphenate their last name.

▶ dance with wolves.

▶ cry with wolves.

▶ take paternity leave, attend pre-natal classes, learn breathing exercises, and wear dummy foetuses strapped to their bellies to "experience what my partner is going through."

▶ wear baby's dried umbilical cord in a locket around their neck.

▶ attend new fathers' re-education gatherings to learn how to be a caring, nurturing, participant father, reveling in the changing of diapers while Mom's off at empowerment seminars.

Fighting Words

"A man would never get the notion of writing a book on the peculiar situation of the human male."
  Simone de Beauvoir,
  The Second Sex, 1949

▶ lactate.

▶ are forever seeing "signs" that the sixties are coming back, and say things like "my son's only 13 but he really digs the Dead."

▶ smile gently and smugly with a studied gentle wisdom whenever provoked.

▶ smile gently and smugly with a studied gentle wisdom for no reason whatsoever other than to be seen as studious, gentle and wise.

▶ read books on how to learn to cry.

▶ sing white middle-class angst songs backed by African/Brazilian/Martian primitives shaking what appear to be hardened goat bladders full of petrified gall stones.

▶ leave the dental practice, drive the Audi to the lake, and spend $850 and forty-eight hours sweating, howling, crawling in mud, cursing their father, coming to terms with feminism, listening to second-rate poetry, and standing around naked with other middle-aged softies until the wild man inside has been apprehended.

▶ learn to reinterpret their fear of physical combat as "a personal contribution towards peace and harmony among all of humankind."

▶ are seen to hug AIDS victims.

▶ become homosexual.

▶ cry.

Workspace

PC	**NOT** *PC*
Sociologist studying violence against women	Sociologist studying violence against non-women
Wildlife photographer	*Hustler* photographer
African Studies professor	White male professor
Male nurse	Female nurse
Witch	Priest

► The Girlishly Correct...

► *celebrate* the hyphenation of their last name.

► double hyphenate their last name (second generation). Hence: Joe Slobowski and Jeannie Higginbottom begot Earth Sibling Higginbottom-Slobowski, who married Sun Spirit Frogley-Dahliwel, in turn begetting little Jennifer Higginbottom-Slobowski-Frogley-Dahliwel, who in a fit of teenaged pique changed her name to Barbi, necessitating immediate victim counselling for mom.

► interpret everyday hardships as a "violation," as in "The *landperson* put shag rug in my apartment. I feel so *violated.*"

Fighting Words

"I sit typing and filing and missing my children. I sit collating accounts — and worried sick about day care. I am writing to Gloria Steinem. 'Dear Gloria, I am going home. I am leaving a job that bores me to become a full-time wife and mother. I have struck a deal with my husband. He will support us while I care for the children. Remind me why this is wrong.'"

Cartoon caption by Jules Feiffer.

▶ interpret any aversion as "feeling threatened," as in, "I feel threatened by this shag rug."

▶ *celebrate* weight gain.

▶ believe aggression is bad unless in the form of *cleansing* female *rage*.

▶ describe the military as "patriarchal war pigs."

- demand a combat role in the army.

- express *hurt and outrage* while demonstrating outside the "paternalistic and exclusionary" men-only club along with their sisters from the women-only shelter.

- seek out perfectly happy women and teach them how to become pitiful victims.

- interpret each and every criticism of feminist dogma as "misogynist."

- *celebrate* taking possession of their first batik tent dress.

- join *free-roaming* campus theater groups that ambush the unsuspecting luncher with "Yes/No comic skits" about sexual assault, that finish with the chorused punchline, "A poisoned environment is any

Trufax

My God, I think I date-raped my car!

A training manual for rape crisis workers at Swarthmore College, Pennsylvania, states that "acquaintance rape spans a spectrum of incidents and behaviors ranging from crimes legally defined as rape to verbal harassment and inappropriate innuendo."

Trufax

Being white didn't help either

When the conservative women's group REAL Women applied to the Canadian government for funding in 1984 using its own name it was ignored. The group applied again using the pseudonym National Association of Lesbian Mothers and was immediately sent the necessary application forms.

situation where sexist comments, gestures, or innuendo exist to degrade women." Proving, once again, that feminists can be entertaining as well as informative.

▶ learn martial arts to defend themselves on dates where innuendo may rear its ugly head.

▶ name their cats for Indian nature goddesses.

▶ hang out at magazine racks to ambush those they see opening *Playboy* and to shriek, "I always wondered what kind of sicko looked at that stuff."

Hot Dates

PC	**NOT** *PC*
Non-competitive Scrabble	Sex
A poetry reading	A dog fight
Bicycling with helmets	Riding a Harley while drunk
Discussion in café	Moist dancing atop car
Swedish movie	Swedish massage

▶ The Romantically Correct...

▶ refer to their boyfriends, girl-friends, husbands or wives, as their "life partner," "spouse," or, if homosexual or similarly sexually challenged, "lover."

▶ greet friends' requests for juicy details about their romance with accounts like "Evan and I have made a commitment to do a couples workshop once a year. It gives us a chance to re-evaluate our relationship and to

talk about the different areas of our life together that have changed, strengthened, or been insufficiently nur-tured . . ."

▶ attend old movies together, wait for politically incorrect dialogue and guffaw loudly to show the rest of us how so perfectly correct they are.

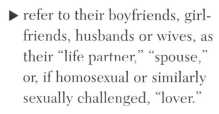

25

Fighting Words

"I think men and women are equal in status. They're just different in function in a marriage relation-ship . . . I also believe that one of my functions is to create a happy atmosphere in the home. I believe that falls to the woman. I can't explain it. I just know that's the way it is."

Marabel Morgan, *The Total Woman* (three million copies sold to the unenlightened)

▶ sends his potential girlfriend a carefully worded "permis-sion" form to sign, clearing the way legally for placement of his arm on her shoulder without fear of reprisal from free-roaming rape crisis lawyers.

▶ are unable to achieve orgasm with a man unless he is on the bottom, bound, broken, whipped and whimpering, "Yes, Mommy, I've been a very naughty white male oppressor and need to be punished."

▶ never expect her to worry about birth control.

▶ prefer their women with body hair.

▶ prefer their men to just leave to them alone.

- ▶ talk earnestly about wanting her to "share the sexual experience."

- ▶ admit to her of "vagina envy" (and weep about it).

- ▶ comfort him, share his tears, and suppress relief when he isn't able to perform.

Trufax

Queer Nation notes

When 50-year-old Portuguese café owner Joe Antunes, of Vancouver, British Columbia, complained about women hugging and kissing each other on his premises, gays and lesbians organized. They took over the cappuccino bar and held a "kiss-in," then moved outside to discourage business by shouting "We're here, we're queer, we don't want your coffee." Antunes retaliated by rigging a sprinkler system to rain on the demonstrators, a move which quickly flushed them away.

▶ The Nurturingly Correct...

▶ bring the baby along to the art gallery/concert/theater.

▶ breast feed in the most public place they can find.

▶ demonstrate their parental mettle by lobbying for state-funded, universal, 24-hour-a-day daycare.

▶ buy their toddlers boring wooden toys.

▶ assiduously devote them-selves to the use of cloth diapers to reduce landfill, meanwhile hiring a diaper service to drive by in its belching, five-mpg truck once a week to cart off the soiled nappies to a laundry where they are washed in non-biodegradable detergent and bleach by underpaid immigrants.

Trufax

And she has a wonderful personality

Cathy Meredig, president of High Self Esteem Toys Corp., of Woodbury, Minnesota, a suburb of Minneapolis, has introduced the "Happy to Be Me Doll." A politically correct alternative to Barbie, the HBM doll is thicker waisted and fatter hipped (36-27-38 vs. 36-18-33), shorter legged and bigger footed, and has nine wardrobes compared to Barbie's more than 100.

▶ phone to congratulate the teacher when their seven-year-old spray paints their leather jacket because, as he had very rightly pointed out, animals do have a "unified psychological presence in the world."

▶ become so stricken when their son flatly refuses to play with his "Eco Warrior" Barbie, and their daughter throws her Greenpeace truck into the vermicomposter, that they are left with little choice but to join a support group.

▶ banish Mother's Day from their kindergarten classes because it is a *repressive symbol of a sexist organization of labor.*

▶ smile indulgently, quoting Rousseau, when their two-and-a-half-year old displays her displeasure by defecating on the floor, strangling the cat, or crushing daddy's testicles.

- have children who write suspiciously precocious letters to the editor expressing "outrage" at the "wanton proliferation of the instruments of annihilation."

- take their kids along on demonstrations to carry signs upon which is scrawled in crayon, "Our wombs are being kidnapped by the state."

- painstakingly explain to their four-year-old how the pea in *The Princess and the Pea* should be interpreted as a symbol that exults clitoral masturbation as a protest of patriarchal sex roles.

- make sure the books they buy little Kirsten or Owl are properly adulterated so that all professionals, laborers and law enforcement personnel are women, while all secretaries, ballerinas, and wet-nurses, men.

Trufax

Babar, black sheep

Patricia Ramsey, director of the Gorse Child Studies Center in Mount Holyoke, Massachusetts, recommends kindergarten teachers avoid Babar (along with many other popular stories) because it "extols the virtues of a European middle-class lifestyle and disparages the animals and people who have remained in the jungle."

▶ become the first on their block to adopt a Third World quadriplegic with AIDS.

▶ don't mind if their children become gay.

▶ provide their teenaged children with condom earrings to proudly wear to school.

▶ cry with their kids.

5 ways to tell your child is being PC'd in school

1 On the day you neglect to place all your cans and bottles in the recycling box, he marches outside your house with a sign reading "My parents are raping our planet."

2 She looks up following your reading of Cinderella and asks, "But didn't she just marry him because she had been brainwashed by patriarchal oppressors?"

3 He begins to object to your swatting of flies on moral grounds.

4 He refuses to play with his Tonka toy trucks and bulldozers because they represent the "phallocentric American desire to conquer nature."

5 She announces that when she grows up she would like to become a lesbian "just like Ms. Beardsley."

City Scape

_PC_	NOT _PC_
San Francisco	Palm Springs
Toronto	Calgary
Havana	Miami
Harare	Cape Town
Oslo	St. Petersburg

▶ The Culturally Correct...

▶ argue that German movies *can* be funny, and pretend to laugh all the way through them, especially at the bits where the young protagonists, looking up for a moment from their Goethe, discover their mothers having sex with their nudist aunts in bathing shelters on North Sea beaches while Elvis sings "Teddy Bear."

▶ recommend to their friends day-long Japanese movies all about people eating.

▶ own several recordings of beluga songs, including some rare 78s.

▶ boast unrelentingly about not having a television.

▶ declare that whilst, yes, they are afraid they do have a television, it's used *purely* for PBS, the single hour per

Fighting Words

"Saying that you did not like Dances With Wolves *or that you disliked* Do the Right Thing, A Dry White Season *or even* My Left Foot *has become socially taboo – a virtual confession of evil-views, including racism, white-supremacist sympathy or contempt for the 'differently abled'. . . . As I discovered the night I proclaimed* Dances With Wolves *'reverential to the point of piety,' 'pedantic' and 'edited' – I was on a roll – 'as if from within a New-Age pot cloud.'"*
Betsy Israel, *American Film*, August, 1991

week of *Sesame Street* they allow their child, and, of course, the occasional *good* German film or *important* documentary.

▶ act as volunteer fund-raisers for PBS subscription drives with the blazing-eyed zeal of Jehovah's Witnesses (but of course without any of the *hateful exclusionary dogma*).

▶ insist that tampon sculptures representing the "toxic shock conspiracy" and audio tape loops of slaughterhouse animals in distress be installed in the local art gallery to replace all those antediluvian daubings by *French oppressionists.*

▶ believe that all inanimate things from the past – quilts, Victorian architecture, bone china, art deco jukeboxes, chastity belts – are intrinsically good, but ensure everyone knows that they certainly don't approve of the *patriarchal systems* that created them.

- attend interdisciplinary theater performances that daringly combine mime, juggling and African nose music to tell the story of several differently abled founding peoples cooperating to collectively nurture a person with AIDS.

- like mimes.

- like jugglers.

- like African nose music.

- attend interminable folk festivals where white, university-educated, city-dwelling, pony-tailed sexagenarians with expensive guitars introduce songs about nuclear reactors with lines like "I got me some ol' country blues I'm a-gonna lay on y'all this mornin'."

- prohibit Eurocentric pictures of African women carrying bananas on their heads, while allowing graphic mixed-media assemblages of sex between women of color and various topical fruits (provided it's done in a tasteful, non-sexist way).

Trufax

The artist as a young dug

Excerpts from a press release advertising shows at the "A Walk Is . . ." art gallery in Vancouver, British Columbia: "Katarina is 'obsessed' with the beauty, sexuality and life force of the female breast. In reading works by womanist writers such as Alice Walker, Maya Angelou and Zora Neale Hurston, she sucks the milk from their giving breasts . . . Katarina paints what she knows. She paints what she wants to see. . . . [Her show] 'I Love Titty' honors the female breast as life-force and sexual focus."

Hit Parade

PC	NOT PC
k. d. lang	Tammy Wynette
Sting	Axl Rose
New Age	Muzak
Tracy Chapman	Paula Abdul
Raffi	Uncle Remus

Movie Tone

PC	**NOT** *PC*
She's Gotta Have It	Deep Throat
Thelma & Louise	Basic Instinct
Kevin Costner	Arnold Schwarzenegger
Jodie Foster	Julia Roberts
Plain popcorn	Jumbo Kit Kat

▶ The Spiritually Correct...

▶ always refer to the God they don't believe in anyway as "She."

▶ describe those who would offer still-pulsating hearts to the Sun God as "practising a different belief system."

▶ write Christmas with a lower case "c."

▶ celebrate *christmas*, not for its connection to a patriarchal belief system, but because of its pagan resonance and ties to the Wicca festival of the winter solstice.

▶ disdain Christians and Jews, but never Buddhists, witches or buffalo dropping worshippers.

▶ revise the Bible in a gender-friendly way, as in "And Abraham hastened into the tent to Sarah, and said, Knead quickly three seahs of wheaten flour, and make cakes. And Sarah said unto Abraham, Thou hast transgressed thy bounds, oh sexist desert pig. And so stressed was she, she hastened to the Human Rights Commission, where she sought empowerment.

And it was good."

▶ profess a divine tolerance for absolutely everyone and everything – except, of course, conservatives, capitalists, Catholics, fundamentalists, hunters, jocks, rednecks, industrialists, policemen, soldiers, smokers, right-to-lifers, Sylvester Stallone, Rotarians, mall merchants, Vanna White, weight-lifters, male judges...

▶ only go to war museums if they've been renamed "peace museums" and re-designed along a war-is-hell theme.

▶ agree with the crude spiritual theories of their young, eg.:
Child: "Nana's not dead, Daddy. Her spirit lives all through the earth – even in our compost bin."
Father: "That sounds about right."

▶ place headphones on their gravid abdomens to soothe, entertain and "educate" a foetus that, under less convenient circumstances, would be considered an amorphous mass of inhuman cells.

▶ organize psychic fairs in the basement of their church to raise money to establish Marxist missions in the Third World.

- celebrate Halloween with home potion-making sessions designed to educate their family in the heritage of those benign and saintly herbologists once known as witches.

- attend only churches that welcome openly gay ministers and worship the black, female, lesbian Christ.

- profess a common kinship with even the lowliest forms of animal life (except Sylvester Stallone, Vanna White, Rotarians, mall merchants. . . .).

Trufax

Atrocities R Us

In 1990 the National Council of Churches (U.S.), refused to acknowledge the 500th Anniversary of Columbus' discovery of America, with the words: "For the descendants of the survivors of the subsequent invasion, genocide, slavery, 'ecocide,' and exploitation of the wealth of the land, a celebration is not an appropriate observance of the anniversary." The Canadian Council of Churches, no doubt eager to demonstrate its moral backbone, said, "If there is any demand from the native peoples of Canada, then we will join them in denouncing 500 years of genocide."

▶ The Gastronomically Correct...

▶ avoid red meat wherever possible, and give testimonials to that effect whenever possible.

▶ use exactly the same tone of voice when speaking about McDonald's or Hitler.

▶ exclaim at how "delightful" that Rainforest Brittle really tastes, and, *Oh, did you know, that all profits go to support small, co-operatively owned Brazil nut processing plants that provide employment for the forest people, but don't destroy any more rainforest, and, of course, it's not sweetened with processed sugar – what do you think we are, suicidal?*

Trufax

Non-human protectors

A waiter and waitress, both in their early twenties and working in a Seattle restaurant, refused to serve a pregnant woman a rum daiquiri. When she persisted in her request, they lectured her on the possible harmful effects of alcohol and read to her the surgeon general's warning about drinking and birth defects.

▶ drink only beer made in a natural way by unionized workers for twice the price.

▶ shun all imbibements from countries with right-of-centre governments.

▶ drink non-caffeinated teas with names coined by persons nostalgic for the drugs that destroyed their minds: "Herbal Sparkle," "Celestial Mindfart," etc.

▶ use chopsticks to eat things better adapted to spoon, fork, fist or Dustbuster.

▶ become active on the anti-Nestlé front.

▶ pathologically use the words "cultural" and "aesthetic" and "dynamic" during loud discussions in restaurants just to spoil everyone else's dinner.

▶ recycle their hummus in their humus toilets.

► have cupboards containing bran, unbleached flour, lentils, honey, lima beans, falafel mix, extra virgin olive oil, dates, brown rice, and rolls of single-ply, chafe-on-contact, melt-in-your-hand toilet paper recycled from old phone books.

Fighting Words

"I gaze walleyed upon a waiter who apologizes fervently that the menu's organic beef isn't completely chemical-free because the supplier's cows have been, by law, vaccinated. Without such vaccination for the last half-century, I counter, our life expectancy might be a good five years less than it is, so that much inorganic I'm happy with. The waiter, who had the immortal certainty of extreme youth on his side, gave me a look of contemptuous compassion. On such occasions I feel that organic terrorism is but a grenade lob away, the pin already drawn."

"Epicure," writing in *Toronto Life*, June 1990

▶ will say loudly to a waiter, "I'll take the deep fried pears stuffed with ripe Camembert on a bed of nutmeg-scented spinach, if you can assure me that no pesticides were used on any of the ingredients," only to grimace, exaggeratedly, when the waiter says the only thing that he possibly could say, which is "What?"

▶ frequent food stores with names like *The Hairy Carrot* or the *Gentle Lentil* that charge an arm and a leg for a wing and a thigh of a "free-ranging" organic chicken nurtured, without antibiotics, on food grown on land purified by New Age shamans with extremely large crystals.

A La Carte

PC	NOT PC
Algae	Kellogg's Frosted Flakes
Lentils	Pork 'n' beans
Muffin	Chocolate cruller
Evian water	Jack Daniels
Veggie burger	Environmentalist (well-cooked)

▶ The Free-Roamingly Correct...

▶ drive Volvos, Subarus, Ladas and/or Saabs – anything dorky looking, not domestic, and, preferably, anything incapable of exceeding the posted speed limit.

▶ drive within the speed limit to "save the planet" and set an example to the rest of the grateful motorists.

▶ wax rhapsodically about public transportation, non-polluting vehicles and car pooling, all the while secretly driving their environmentally murderous Microbus to work, having signed the latest petition to keep Light Rapid Transit out of the heritage neighborhood they inhabit.

▶ expose their bodies on nude beaches as though they were still at Woodstock and everyone else was still too zonked to be sickened by their white and wattled flesh.

▶ delight in pronouncing all foreign place names in an exaggerated accent of origin, particularly when it involves the excessive and offensive overproduction of mucus (e.g., Nicaragua = Nischsks harrrrr ogggg oooo a).

▶ wear ridiculous plastic armour and tiny rear-view helmet mirrors while pedalling $1,500 mountain bikes around quiet suburban crescents.

▶ have "never bothered" to earn drivers' licenses – and are insistently proud of the fact.

▶ cross-country ski, hike, cycle, snowshoe, kayak, canoe, speed-walk.

- ▶ do not downhill ski, stock-car race, motorcycle, Winnebago, speedboat or fly their own plane.

- ▶ spend four perfectly good vacation weeks trekking through leech bogs in Nepal.

- ▶ return from vacations bearing yet more specimens to add to their extensive collection of "birth sculptures."

Fighting Words

"The 'carers' no doubt think of themselves as liberals, but they are, of course, fascists trying to stamp out the few pleasures left to the rest of the population. It's impossible to eat without finding oneself lectured by some jerk on the evils of salt, meat, fat, sugar or monosodium glutamate. Places to light up a calming cigar are thinner on the ground than signs of upturn in the economy. People regularly bang on the window of the Roller to complain about its fuel consumption while one takes one's life in one's hands when one ventures out in the winter wrapped up, as nature intended, in a comfortable fur coat."

Oofy Prosser, *Punch*,
Jan. 8–14, 1992

Affirmative Action

► The Academically Correct...

► refuse to believe history written by "dead white males" (a.k.a. DWMs).

► dismiss all literature written by "dead white males" (except Karl Marx).

► reject art painted by "dead white males."

► revere anything written, drawn or tapped out on tom-toms by physically and mentally challenged street kids taught by inner-city kindergarten teacher collectives. Why? Because it's *valid*.

► elevate the *self-esteem* of black students by teaching them how Africans, disguised as Egyptians, invented civilization roughly 5,000 years

Fighting Words

"The eagle never lost so much time as when he submitted to learn of the crow."

William Blake
(Dead White Male)

before the birth of Christ (a distant ancestor of Malcolm X), spread it to the rest of the world by crossing the Alps on elephants; sired Napoleon; colonized the Americas; wrote all the great symphonies; defeated Nazism; put the first man on the Moon; and invented Velcro.

▶ refer in low, reverential tones to the lowliest, most ineffectual dogpatch teacher as an "educator."

▶ strive to eliminate the "phallocentricity" from literature, while wondering disingenuously just what on earth is wrong with *Moby Ovum* as a book title anyway.

▶ encourage and subsidize any text book that depicts any white explorer of the New World as a bull-whip-toting, Hitlerian papoose-stomper, while portraying the aboriginal folk as gentle, peace-loving, guitar-plucking proto-Marxists, who would no sooner shoot an arrow at a fellow than take his scalp.

- eschew the word "Oriental" in favour of "Asian-American", to the utter disinterest of most Oriental students who are too busy aceing everyone else to care about what the silly "round eyes" call them.

- insist that engineering students caught watching strippers undergo *rehabilitation and education* by being forced to escort lesbians home from late-night Goddess-in-Everywoman seminars.

Trufax

Reaching out to women in the heterocentric dance arts

The University of British Columbia, whose engineers are notorious for their heterosexual exuberance, has started a course entitled "Society and the Engineer," which covers such topics as sexual harassment, multiculturalism, employment equity, and the "impact major engineering projects have had on Native Canadians." The dean of applied science said the course just shows how "the engineering profession is actively reaching out to people."

Trufax

Will ya look at the forest management rodent on her!

A professor at the University of California at Santa Barbara, after telling students that the preferred PC term for pet was "companion animal," mused that Penthouse Pet centerfolds might become Penthouse Companion Animals. Fifteen women promptly filed sexual harassment charges.

▶ adopt the language of fellow PCers in the silly sciences, as in, "Your *siblings* may be *physically challenged*, but that should not prevent you from *assuming the role of care-giver and nurturer*, so as to *provide them with* a suitably *child-centered, gender-neutral environment*, thus enhancing their *self-esteem.*" – without even cracking a smile.

▶ spend university reading weeks attending Lesbian/ Bisexual Awareness activities.

▶ seek victim counselling because of the stress caused by worrying if the dean's job was awarded her for reasons of talent or because she was the only quadriplegic of color who could be found.

Fashion Sense

PC	NOT PC
Alpaca	Cashmere
Mountain Co-op	Saks Fifth Avenue
Granny glasses	Contact lenses
Batik	Mink
Plastic coffee cup on rope	Pearl-handled revolver
Curry comb	Lady Schick

▶ The Stereotypically Correct...

▶ use the words fascist and conservative interchangeably, especially when speaking of *Korporate Amerika.*

▶ re-invent words every generation to avoid their meaning until there are no more words to use and the originals return. Hence: colored person-negro-black-Afro-American-person of color.

▶ are forever asking "how do you *feel?*"

▶ react to any suggestion that welfare recipients might be encouraged to scck work with a shudder, a long, condescending groan, and a patronizing rejoinder involving repetition of the word "simplistic."

▶ actively lobby to make sports teams change their "racially inappropriate" names to things like the Washington Oppressors.

Trufax

That's just nuts

The Philadelphia Federation of Teachers, wishing to avoid the hopelessly ablist term disabled, set up a "Committee for Teachers with Special Needs." They found that didn't work when a bum walked in saying he had a "special need" for housing. Hence it became the "Committee for Members who are Physically Challenged." But a timorous fifth-grade teacher appeared, thinking it was a support group for instructors intimidated by students. Today it's known as the "Committee for Disabled Members."

The Stereotypically Correct...

▶ boast about never having been inside one of "those shopping malls."

▶ quote Swedish statistics relentlessly and with an awful wistfulness.

▶ are vehemently anti-tobacco (*Well, who isn't these days?*) and post witty signs in their home like "We have a smoking room. It's outside."

▶ use metric measure as a matter of principle.

▶ call a spade a "non-organic earth-moving tool of the genocidal white settler."

▶ nod maniacally, as if hyperventilating with ecstasy, at parties when another PC says something like-minded, such as "I used to be a stockbroker, but I didn't know anything about what really went on in life, you know? Now I'm a communication facilitator at a holistic healing-arts center. I like it here on the coast. Everything's so acceptable."

▶ stay awake nights wrestling with such dilemmas as whether protesting of furs is hurtful to the livelihood of founding peoples, whether it's fair to keep one's children in the ceramics-oriented public school system or put them in private school so they will learn to read, whether multiculturalism encourages wife-burning by immigrant husbands, whether or not to attend the Newport Folk festival this year now that it's being sponsored by Nestlé. . . .

▶ bring in a combined professional net income of $250,000 a year, own a $50,000 Volvo and a $60,000 Range Rover, live in a $500,000 cedar home, take academically guided cruises to Antarctica, send their children to $5,000-a-year "open learning" schools, sail a $200,000 sailboat, and declaim that the world has "gone mad with greed and consumerism."

Fighting Words

"Political correctness isn't just good liberal intentions run amok...It is racism and, for that matter, sexism . . . Accept that only blacks can teach African history or that only men can be sexist and you are not very far from accepting that blacks have rhythm, that women make lousy drivers, and that Jews are good with money."

Lorrie Goldstein, writing in the *Toronto Sun*, 1991

Fighting Words

"I don't trust people who claim to like Central American folk songs better than everything they hear on the radio. I don't think they're lying; I just think they're dullards." Steven Perry, writing in *City Pages,* a Minneapolis-St. Paul left-wing weekly.

Role Models

PC	**NOT** *PC*
Karl Marx	Jesus Christ
Gloria Steinem	Virgin Mary
Gro Brundtland	Margaret Thatcher
Greg Louganis	Mike Tyson
Anita Hill	Long Dong Silver
Mom	Dad

PC SPEAK

▶▶

*Dictionary of the
Devilish Tongue*

PC SPEAK	TRANSLATION	UNACCEPTABLE
Aboriginal Land Claims	Indian legal claim to approximately twice the area of North America	Sour grapes
Afraid of closeness	Unable to become romantic drinking herbal tea and listening to Tracy Chapman records	Granolaphobia
Afro-American	Black	Negro
AIDS	Celebrity-sanctioned, predominantly homosexual disease	*Dee-viiine* retribution

Trufax

. . . Not to mention all those kindly crack dealers

Leonard Jeffries, chairman of the Black Studies department at City College, New York City, and an extreme exponent of Afrocentricism, divides the human race into "ice people" and "sun people." The ethnic groups descended from the ice people are materialistic, selfish, and violent, while those descended from the sun people are non-violent, cooperative, and spiritual. In addition, blacks are biologically superior to whites, Jeffries maintains, having more melanin, which regulates intellect and health.

PC SPEAK	TRANSLATION	UNACCEPTABLE
Alternative, alternate lifestyle	PC-approved living	Welfare
Anti-smoking bylaws	San Francisco-originated scheme for oppressing 30 per cent of the population	Smokism
Art	The modern forum for complaint	Applied welfare
Asian	Oriental	Boss
Belief system	PC-sanctioned religion	Paganism

PC SPEAK	TRANSLATION	UNACCEPTABLE
Bovine citizenry	Unenlightened masses, non-PCers, mall goers, television watchers and worse	Us
Canola	Softer, gentler term for rapeseed	Sexual assault seed
Caring profession	Any occupation taken by a PCer	The victim sciences
Chair, chairperson	Chairman, chairwoman	Chaircreature
Childcare	Daycare	Early childhood indoctrination

Metaphorically Correct

"Judging by both our crowded shopping malls and aberrant public opinion polls, the electronic shepherd has driven a bovine citizenry far from the theatre of ideas, deep into the binary logic of the marketplace. With things going so delightfully for those on the fast and loose track, it is little wonder that they try to cement their position by raising the specter of 'political correctness' to attack what few clusters of antibodies still lurk in the body politic."

Uku Kasemets, described as "cartoonist and writer," in the *Toronto Star*, June 11, 1991.

69

Trufax

What red flag would that be?

In writing a letter about her reservations about attending a University of Pennsylvania "diversity education" session, a freshman student happened to mention her "deep regard for the individual." A university administrator, writing back, underlined the word "individual" and explained, "This is a RED FLAG phrase today, which is considered by many to be RACIST. Arguments that champion the individual over the group ultimately privilege the 'individuals' belonging to the largest or dominant group."

PC SPEAK	TRANSLATION	UNACCEPTABLE
Child-centered	Type of education where the child decides the study	Kiddy-whipped
Community	PC-approved Establishment i.e., "Gay Community"	Coven
Confusion	What one is experiencing if swayed by a non-PC argument	Enlightenment
Consciousness raising	The imparting of PC verities on the impressionable	Re-education

PC SPEAK	TRANSLATION	UNACCEPTABLE
Culturally distinct inner-city community	Ghetto	Crack Alley
Differently abled (also: otherly abled, handicapable, uniquely abled, physically challenged, inconvenienced)	Crippled, deformed, mentally retarded	PC mascot material
Diversity	Victimhood	Tyranny
Date rape, acquaintance rape	"Any sexual intercourse without mutual desire."	Sex with a feminist

Fighting Words

"From what I can see, the end they seek is the removal of all language that brings to anyone's mind a negative or in any form degrading image. Is this possible? Can any language be written so 'correctly' as to invoke only pleasant or neutral feelings?...With the removal of terms of derision, will the prejudices also disappear — or will these new terms adopt connotations that users of the old terms may have seen in those terms."

Dennis F. Chiappetta, a Syracuse, N.Y., law student, in a letter to the *New York Times Magazine*, May 5, 1991

PC SPEAK	TRANSLATION	UNACCEPTABLE
Dead White Male (DWM)	(derog.) a creator of Western Civilization	God
Demeaning	Disliked by feminists	Male
Discrimination	Hiring for merit	Discriminating
Empowerment	Successful affirmative action	Revenge of the nerds
Establishment	The politically incorrect community	Us

PC SPEAK	TRANSLATION	UNACCEPTABLE
Eurocentric	Favoring European history and custom	Civilized
Exceptional	Slow learning	Dumb
Environmentalist	Outraged pop scientist	White urban sentimentalist
Fascist (also: reactionary, antediluvian, troglodyte, Neanderthal)	Non PCer (also see: bovine citizenry)	Us
Feel	Preferred alternative to "think"	Grok

Trufax

Wo . . . wo . . . wo

In their 1987 book Teaching Children Sensitivity, *authors Linda and Richard Eyre advise, "Use the word 'feel' — both in telling and in asking (to help children become more generally aware of your feelings and of theirs). As you form the habit of saying 'I feel,' also form the habit of asking 'How do you feel?'. . . Move away from asking children so many 'why,' 'when,' and 'where' questions and start asking more 'how do you feel about' questions. Encourage children to identify their feelings and express them to you, and praise every effort they make to talk about their feelings."*

PC SPEAK	TRANSLATION	UNACCEPTABLE
Feminist	Something a man will call himself late at night, if necessary, to facilitate sex	Fembo
Free-roaming protector	Wild animal	Meat
Funding	Government subsidy received by PCers	Hush money
Gender enhancement	Affirmative action	Cheating

PC SPEAK	TRANSLATION	UNACCEPTABLE
Gender feminist	Type who won't rest until the family stands in ruins and men are no longer needed for reproduction	Pit bull
Gender neutral	Favoring neither male or female	Sexless
Green (n.)	PCer from West Coast	Sapsucker
Green (adj.)	Any product foul-tasting, unattractive, or inconvenient	Brownish

Trufax

First, men are persuaded to do the laundry, then . . .
Classified Advertisement in Harrow-smith, *the "magazine for country living":* MANY MOONS WASHABLE *menstrual pads. Pads $34 plus $3 S & H. Specify velcro wings or belted style. Select soft or wild pattern. Ecofem. Mississauga, ON.*

Fighting Words

"Finally, as a public service, here is how a few familiar books and movies might be translated into modspeak:

- Beauty and the Beast – *A Lookism Survivor and a Free-roaming Fellow Mammal*
- War and Peace — *Violence Processing and the Temporary Cessation of Hostilities.*
- Three Blind Mice – *A Triad of Visually Impaired, Wall-dwelling Protectors*
- Old Yeller – *Senior Animal Companion of Color*
- Snow White and the Seven Dwarfs – *One of the Monocultural Oppressed Womyn Confronts the Vertically Challenged*
- Men at Arms – *The Myn Are at It Again."*

John Leo, *U.S. News & World Report*, July 29, 1991

PC SPEAK	TRANSLATION	UNACCEPTABLE
Heritage language	PC-favored language, preferably from Third World	Pig Spanish
Herstory	Women's history	An easy credit
Hispanic Butcher, the	Christopher Columbus	Discoverer of America
Homophobic	Critical of homosexuality	Straight
Homemaker	Housewife	Mom
Hurtful	Adjective applied to anything inimical to PCthink	Heartfelt

PC SPEAK	TRANSLATION	UNACCEPTABLE
Important (author, artist, restaurant, etc., etc.)	Politically correct	Second-rate
Inappropriately directed laughter	Laughing at PCs	Slapstick
Installation	PC art work	Glued garbage with an attitude
Latinos	Hispanics	Sons of Columbus
Linear	(derog.) Logical	Scientific
Logocentric	(derog.) Favoring articulate expression	Fluent

PC Speak at Work

Three persons of color were pedalling their bicycles up a steep hill when they decided to dismount and hitchhike. Before long a truck carrying bowling balls stopped and the driver — a woman — stopped and bade the persons of color get in the back amongst the bowling balls with their bikes. Going down the other side of the hill, the truck exceeded the legal speed limit and was stopped by two police officers — women, naturally. Looking in the back of the truck, one police officer said to the other, "Goddess! It's a truck full of person-of-color eggs and three of them have hatched."

"Yes," remarked the other, "and they've already unlawfully obtained bicycles!"

PC SPEAK	TRANSLATION	UNACCEPTABLE
Lookism	Bias based on appearance	Aesthetics
Magisteriate	Non-sexist term for master's degree	Baby doc
Matriarchal societies	Women-ruled societies	Feminist mythology
Misogynist (also: gynophobe)	Any male who argues with a feminist	Any male
Mobility challenged, the	Deconstructionist term for antebellum black slaves	Bucks 'n' Mammies

PC SPEAK	TRANSLATION	**UNACCEPTABLE**
Multiculturalism	The worship of minorities	Racism with a heart (and funding)
New Age	PC-related movement created by sixties survivors too drug damaged to infiltrate the professions	Synaptically challenged
New Historicist	Proponent of reconstructed history, e.g. Cleopatra was black, the only "Greats" are female Latinos, Alberta Schweitzer was a racist, etc.	Impossibilist

Trufax

Women finally make gains in science

Lewis Lapham, editor of Harper's, *writes of a literary agent he knows who has boasted of his daughter's correctness. Asked by her private-school biology teacher to look through a microscope at bacteria in a drop of water, the 15-year-old girl refused, saying that although the creatures might be weak, simple and under-represented politically, she would not infringe on their right to privacy. After a moment of apparently stunned silence, the teacher congratulated the girl for her civil disobedience, told her that of course she didn't have to look at the bacteria, and thanked her for teaching the class a lesson that couldn't be learned from a microscope.*

PC SPEAK	TRANSLATION	UNACCEPTABLE
Non-human companion (also: protector)	Pet	Andrea Dworkin
Nurture	Raise	Spoil
Ombudsman	Exalted member of PC clergy who conducts witch hunts against non-believers	Captain Kangaroo
Opportunity hiring	Affirmative action	Discrimination
Oppressor	Anyone higher on the hierarchical ladder	Better

PC SPEAK	TRANSLATION	UNACCEPTABLE
Organically grown	Grown without pesticides	Scabby & diseased
PCPs	Politically Correct Persons	Toxic substances
Paranoid Right, the	See fascist, etc.	On to their game
Parent (v.)	Raise	Spoil
Persons of Color	Non-whites	Coloreds
Phallocentric	Believing males were largely responsible for civilization	Cocksure
Pre-woman	Little girl	Boy-hater

Fighting Words

"It's fascism of the left. These people behave like the Hitler Youth."
Camille Paglia, iconoclastic feminist author of *Sexual Personae*

81

Fighting Words

"These codes punishing verbal harassment are patronizing and paternalistic. The 'protection' they promise is incapacitating…The imputation is that there is some inherent genetic weakness — a black genetic weakness on my part. And that's why codes of conduct are needed to protect me. That is the most insulting, the most racist statement of all."

Alan Keyes, debating Stanford University speech code architect Tom Grey

PC SPEAK	TRANSLATION	UNACCEPTABLE
Progressive	PC-approved	Scabby & diseased
Racist!	Epithet hurled at anyone expressing non PC-approved opinions, in non-PC-approved language	Clarence Thomas
Rape Crisis Center	Feminist-staffed haven for the victims of rape and other sexist acts	Recruitment office

PC SPEAK	TRANSLATION	UNACCEPTABLE
Self-esteem, self-actualization, self-realization, etc.	PC state of grace; what can be achieved if the funding is available	Self love
Sell out	Veer from the PC path	Grow up
Sexist (adj.)	Traditionally male	Manly
Sexist (n.)	Traditional male	Dad
Simplistic	Arguments PCers oppose but cannot answer	Succinct

Trufax

Non-human companions present may also have suffered

In 1990, a committee at the University of Toronto defined sexual harassment as behavior "which emphasizes the sex or sexual orientation of one or more individuals in a manner which the actor knows, or ought reasonably to know, creates, or could reasonably be expected to create, an intimidating, hostile or offensive environment for persons of that sex or sexual orientation and/or for persons present at that occurrence."

PC SPEAK	TRANSLATION	UNACCEPTABLE
Sizist	Judging a person by his weight	The difference between a feminist and a whale? Fifty pounds and a plaid shirt.
Social conscience	What PCers have and others don't	Pity to burn
Speciesism	Favouring one species (say, humans) over another (say, algae)	Pest control

PC SPEAK	TRANSLATION	UNACCEPTABLE
Substance abuser	Wino, junkie	PC fugitive
Survivor (as in, substance abuse survivor)	Victim	Instant saint
Task force, action committee	PC body seeking public money	Political welfare bums
Third World	Under-developed countries suffering from a lack of Marxist government	NOT CUBA!

PC SPEAK	TRANSLATION	UNACCEPTABLE
To know is to fuck	Unlady-like gender-feminist battle cry, meaning all existing knowledge is *androcentric* and therefore just another form of rape	And the same to you, madam
Valid	Supporting PC precepts	Pallid
Vegan	Extreme form of vegetarian who shuns eggs and dairy products, as well as meat	Ruminant

PC SPEAK	TRANSLATION	UNACCEPTABLE
Victim (also: disempowered)	Recently discredited term for the weak and unpopular who make up the PC leaders' constituency	*Les Misérables*
Violence against women	Anything from an unwanted wink to murder to rape	Primary feminist industry
Wellness	Health with granola on its breath	Shamanism
Women's Studies	University department invented to spread feminist propaganda	Witches & Goddesses 101

Fighting Words

"The weak are the most treacherous of us all. They come to the strong and drain them. They are bottomless. They are insatiable. They are always parched and always bitter. They are everyone's concern and like vampires they suck our life's blood."
    Bette Davis,
    The Lonely Life, 1962

Bumper Shtick

PC

NOT PC

PC	NOT PC
Save our Planet	When you're hungry and out of work, eat an environmentalist
Trees Are for Loving	Log it, burn it, pave it
If you love something set it free, if it comes back, etc., etc.	If you love something, set it free. If it doesn't come back, hunt it down and kill it
Women make great leaders, you're following one now	I ❤ my Oriental wife
Mothers against drunk drivers	I may be slow, but I'm shit-faced